All Is Love: the Pet Solution

Dr. Sally Nazari

ISBN: 9781696459563

DEDICATION

With the deepest, unwavering gratitude and love to my heart, and my Angel, and my forever Queen LaLa, whose contributions to the fulfillment of this pursuit extend so far beyond joy, affection, and enthusiasm.

CONTENTS

ACKNOWLEDGMENTS

Also a note of acknowledgement for my beloved furry-footed

family and friends whose devotion and support

have helped turn this once lifelong dream

into a shared reality -- Taura, Archie, Kingy, Lucky, Lucy, Zsa,

Zsa, Philip, and Lucifer.

1 INTRODUCTION TO THE HUMAN-ANIMAL BOND

Have you ever looked down on a certain pet and thought of such an animal as being just an ordinary animal? Let me assure you: you are in for a shocker if you share this opinion. Research has shown that about 71million American households (which stands at a staggering 62 percent) live with a pet. It is quite inaccurate to assume that pets are not important. In fact, pets can do as much as people can do when it comes to helping other people mentally and emotionally.

This transformative relationship didn't begin in modern times. It actually began as far back as in the 18th century with William Turke who ran an asylum confirming that his patients gained tremendous mental health benefits from being around animals like rabbits, poultry animals, sea bulls and so on. In the 21st century, there is a wider range of animals that can serve as pets and help us immensely in both cases of mental health issues and in everyday living. Birds, dogs, fish, cats, horses, rabbits are all a part of the very long list of animals that offer tremendous help to humans in various ways. Pets can get us through tough situations like breakups, loss of a loved one, illnesses, you name it! The list is, as many of us with beloved pets know, seemingly bulky.

Perhaps you have even wondered why some folks are almost inseparable from their pets. Often, it is reported that this is because such lovely animals can serve as a companion, friend, a confident among other things. This book will take a microscopic look at the relationship between these lovely pets and humans. Our pets provide happiness, fulfillment, company, and irrefutable love - among the numerous things needed emotionally by humans for longevity and sanctity of life. In the following chapters, we will take a look into the human-animal symbolic interaction including people's intersection with their non-human best friend- the dog. Canines have been involved in ensuring the mental stability in many people. Among many other things, dogs ensure companionship and security for us and they love us unconditionally. Many families see their pets as a part of their family as they help in reducing stress, anxiety and depression. These medical/health benefits cannot be overemphasized but they are not the only reasons to live with a pet. There are also other physical and social benefits as pets (especially dogs) can help us stay fit by making you go on walks and runs with them or they with us. Many have reported that, in this process, they have enhanced their social connections by forming relationships with various people.

Also, together, we will take a look at the canine assisted treatment of trauma, and other emotional ailments like depression, as well as how these lovely canines and other pets have helped survivors to improve both their internal and external worlds. They help survivors to deal with issues of their self-perception and an inability to trust others which requires, in most cases, the service of skilled interventions to address and help conquer. With this in mind, it is generally necessary to recreate avenues through which such people can connect with others, feel empowered, and revive hope in their lives. This is where canines come in, through the possible integration of canines in the provision of psychotherapy to individuals trying to cope with the impact of trauma exposure. Happily for us, dogs are uniquely suited for such powerful transformations. People grappling with the effects of trauma are helped to overcome such ailments and survivors of complex trauma often undergo significant personality changes and post-traumatic stress disorders (PTSD) and this might eventually lead to substance abuse, mood disorders, dis-associative disorders and so on.

Perhaps, a particular type of clinical experience that could offer these individuals a means for learning to rebuild their capacity to interact and connect more effectively with others might be the integration of animals in trauma recovery work. Animal-based clinical interventions may provide therapeutic gains I certain areas like isolation, hyper-arousal, sense of security, disempowerment, avoidance and mistrust. One possible result may be that individuals encountering these distressing effects following traumatic exposure may benefit from clinical interventions that focus upon the use of animals in order to help in providing symptom relief and acquisition of more adaptive coping strategies to better aid their recovery from these ailments. In the USA, the first documented use of animals therapeutically occurred in New York during world war 2 at an air corps convalescent hospital for 'operational fatigue' which is closely matched with what we call post-traumatic stress disorder (PTSD). And canines were predominantly enlisted. These efforts to include canines in the treatment for mental illness continued throughout the 19th century and then in the 20th century, these efforts became much more formal, structured and intentional.

The man who was dubbed the father of animal based therapies noticed the rapport building skills of his own companion canine while working with a patient who was particularly guarded. He continued this work and though it wasn't well re-

ceived, his primary theoretical principles explicating his observations relied upon ego psychology-based notions that traumatized human beings
had become alienated from connections with others and with nature. In the 1970's, Samuel and
Elizabeth Corson also introduced the assistance of
canines into mental healthcare within a psychiatric facility and a nursing home where they concluded observational and empirical studies that
patients previously unresponsive to other treatment showed increased social interactions and
improved patient- staff relations. Their works
greatly influenced others and this reflects in the
fact that further studies were conducted and the
results were very similar to the original and it
also had its own additional findings which
showed that canines helped patients to relief
stress and enhance cardiovascular health through
interaction with dogs.

Shortly thereafter, the Delta Society, founded in 1977 by a group of medical and veterinary
professionals spear-headed the exploration of animal integration into interventions targeted toward the well-being of humans. The organization
also focused on training, certifying, and registering therapy and service dogs in addition to prioritizing research on the human-animal interventions. Through these efforts, they began structuring animal-assisted interventions by describing
group and individual interventions as well as several benefits of therapeutic use of canines. Some

of these advantages were outlined to include such things as training canines to assist in medical crises by dialing emergency services or fetching medications, helping individuals with panic disorders and agoraphobia to venture out into the world, helping to ground and orient individuals with dissociative disorders, facilitating emotional reactivity through grounding strategies provided through physical contact, and alerting individuals with an exaggerated startle response when people are approaching. Assistance such as this likely contributes to a sense of security and safety as well as potentially facilitates feelings of empowerment in humans.

Because animals are potentially less likely to trigger trauma reactions and may revitalize a sense of hope in reconnecting with one's world, as discussed below, they might offer a unique pathway toward accessing the implicit memories involved in recovery from traumatic symptoms and the journey to recovery and rediscovery. Thus, employment of the possible unique effects that animals such as canines may elicit might offer valuable components of facilitating enduring changes in the challenges that survivors of trauma and even everyday humans encounter in both their internal and external worlds. This books looks to examine not only the features of traumatic symptoms, but also the potential healing and perhaps beneficial aspects of the human-animal bond and animal-facilitated/assisted therapy with a particular emphasis on ways that such therapy may possibly enact potentially effective and perhaps lasting changes to possibly alleviate these symptoms. Perhaps effectively structuring canine involvement in psychotherapy for the recovery of trauma responses could offer a greater likelihood of achieving this intent, since canines may bring with them an advanced social acumen and projections of non-judgment and empathy that might better enable not just healing but also ensures the prevention of mental issues generally in humans.

A descriptive study targeting mental health practitioners across the nation yielded similar findings. A random sampling of 5,012 social workers self-identified as providers of direct clinical care were distributed a survey comprised of 38 questions using a Likert scale targeted to address areas of the inclusion of companionate animals as part of assessment and treatment in their clinical work, exposure to training and knowledge of the human-animal bond, and their training in the use of animals throughout their mental health training. The final sample yielded a response rate of 33 percent, with 1,649 respondents. Based on descriptive data from the respondents, 1,091 mental health practitioners include questions about companionate and other animals as part of their assessments, while 381 include animals as part of their interventions. Among these practitioners, the most commonly used animal, with an n of 320, was the dog. Respondents also overwhelmingly reported no training in the inclusion of companionate or other animals in their practice, with 1,621 or 95.7 percent of respondents reporting this. A mere 12.6 percent of respondents reported special training on animal assisted therapies. It is important to consider that such a large disparity amongst practitioners with training and those without training might be indicative of problematic practices. Furthermore, of the total respondents, 79.3 percent stated that they would like more training on the human animal bond. Based on the respondents' information, Risley-Curtiss postulated that while animals were perceived by her sample to be a part of human beings' ecologies and need to be included in the clinical system to significantly enhance the well- being of clients, more than two-thirds of the practitioners did not ask about the role of relationships with animals.

Perhaps one of the several challenges to this practice occurring may include a lack of specialized education and training. It might be particularly important for individuals with such debilitating and pervasive issues to be treated by professionals with adequate training in the provision of mental health treatment to ensure the likelihood of competent and skilled treatment delivery. This training is only necessary when it comes to the professional use of canines and other pets in treating mental issues but when it comes to the prevention of metal issues and the enhancement of one's life through the use of the human-animal bond, no training is necessary as it is in a pet's nature to love unconditionally and help to stabilize the mental health of his/her adopted owner.

2 WHY DO I NEED A PET?

In the evolution of man and animal relationship (in this case pets) there has been a particularly significant change in the way that man relates with animals particularly his pets. Overtime, the relationship has advanced from that of fear of being prey to genuine friendship between man and pets. I will be viewing the importance of pets generally but I will occasionally branch out and focus on the dog's importance to man as man's best friend. Most of the valid points in the defense of the closeness of the dog to man are closely related and occasionally similar to that of other pets therefore I might occasionally use them interchangeably.

In both the United states and Australia, a staggering 63% of households include pets and although the number varies from one country to another but this doesn't take away from the fact that pets are a very important part of our lives. How are pets important to our lives? The rest of this chapter will look to answer that question.

As humans, we are built psychologically to care about someone or something else apart from ourselves and depending on the degree humans tend to gain a lot of satisfaction from being responsible for the proper upbringing of another being or the successful completion of one endeavor or another. This is evident in the fact that most people become more responsible wh0en they have a new kid because of the joy that comes with nurturing and caring for another being. Caring for a pet ca give that form of fulfilment to people who do not have kids yet (for whatever reasons) or for the older folks who have grown up kids who are leading their lives already. Having a pet in this type of situation helps such a person to fill in the space of having a companion or friend. This can act as a huge psychological boost for such persons.

Another common advantage of pets, particularly canines is that they provide a sense of security to most humans. Most people feel more secured when they have their canine around them. Also pets can sense danger and prevent it, there have been numerous cases where dogs have been said to prevent danger or alerted their owners and saved the from fire outbreaks and other similar incidents. Pets like parrots can also be very helpful in similar situations and can go a long way to ensure the total safety of their owners. Because pets love genuinely, they will always go an extra mile to ensure that a pet owner is never too stressed in that they reduce the stress level immensely because playing with a pet increases the brain's level of dopamine and serotonin (both are associated closely with pleasure). Next time you feel stressed for whatever reason and you need to relax then I strongly suggest that you get yourself a pet that will keep you happy and take away stress.

If you have never taken out time to notice, then the next time you are in a home with kids that own pets or teenagers and adults that grew up with pets. You will notice that they would probably not have issues with self-esteem and they will handle stress better (notice that I used the word "probably" because it is not always the case and there are exceptions). More often than not, pets improve the self-esteem in a child and helps them to be better equipped mentally to tackle issues that are stressed related. Pets can also reduce stress in the workplace and as studies have shown that having your pet present in your workplace can help immensely in the reduction of stress

Pets are also very important in the sense that they can successfully act as an 'antidote' for loneliness because through regular interactions with a pet, a bond (that cannot be easily broken) is built. It also helps to talk to one's pets when you feel the need to talk about things that bother you as it has been psychologically proven to help in the reduction of anxiety, sadness and stress. Pets tend to love their owners unconditionally and care for them. This sense of being loved helps tremendously in improving the mood of a pet owner and there have been several cases of pets especially dogs going through unbelievable hurdles to reconnect with their owners in cases of a physical disconnect. For a lot of pet owners, their pets give them a reason to look forward to another day. These little (or sometimes huge) pets lessen a pet owner's chances of being depressed or lonely because pets will not only help you mentally but physically and health-wise as I would look into subsequently in this chapter but for now let us take a look at a a couple of things that can be learnt from owning pets.

Firstly, being a pet owner apart from all the other amazing things teaches compassion which you would agree is key in ensuring a great life. How exactly does owning a pet affect our level of compassion? Compassion for others is developed when you have to look outside your own wants and needs and consider others. When you own a pet, you learn to be more compassionate and then you do a lot of compromising. For example, if you really need to stay home to see a basketball game and your pet on the other hand really wants to go for a walk then you might have to check for regular updates on your mobile device. This is a way of becoming compassionate about another being. Permit me to say that having a pet will teach you almost the same level of compassion (well, assuming that there exists a suitable scale to measure compassion). Summarily, Pets can teach you a thing or two about compassion.

Another very important thing that can be learned from owning a pet isn't the ability to read non-verbal communication. The fact that your pet cannot speak (except you own a parrot) is initially a challenge but with time, you begin to get used and it is amazing how this skill can be transferred to your daily interactions with other humans and pets. It has been widely speculated that close to 90% of communication is non-verbal therefore you can understand certain gestures and body language based on your regular non-verbal communication with your pet. Once this skill is perfectly mastered, then you have become a body language reader without picking up a book on psychology and this can help you secure huge points in school, church, in the corporate world and so on. Asides that, dogs can also provide details about your personality. This can be done by evaluating the kinds of pet you like/keep. For example, if like 47% of American pet owners, you choose to own a dog then you are probably more extroverted, more agreeable and more conscientious than folks that own cats. On the other hand, in America, 37% of American homes own at least a cat and a certain study showed that folks that own cats tend to be more creative, adventurous and are very open people. Also cats owners have been said to be smarter than dog owners and even though fewer families own cats, mostly cat lovers

have more than one cat. The most independent set
of pet owners are the ones that own reptiles, un-
fortunately they are the least humorous. These
and more are the kinds of things you will learn
about a person based on the type of pet the person
owns.

Your pet can also help you improve your social
interaction that is if you have issues relating to
other people then your pet can provide adequate
relation with other pet owners/admirers and people in general. By walking with your pet to your
local park, you can form lasting relationships
with other pet own0ers while your pet might also
make new friends. In doing this, dogs and other
pets can help owners to overcome being shy and
also help them to better express themselves.
Also, pets can also help in the process of recovery from an event you would rather not want to
remember like the loss of a loved one or the end
of a relationship among other displeasing events.
This is more pronounced with cats but other pets
too can help you to look forward with hope and
leave the past behind. Pets can also help you find
your partner as they can help foster relationships
between humans.
Some pets have heightened sense of smell, sight
and hearing which means that they can help immensely when it comes to sensing things happen-
ing around. Pets like cats have been found to be
attractive to a lot of women, so much so that

some women would rather sleep side-by-side with their pets than their partners, this has been proven through researches and polls.

Pets can save your life, yes they can, here I will highlight ways that these animals can save/preserve your health.

Firstly, studies have shown that talking to your pet and playing with it comes with reduced blood pressure and heart rates which reduces the need to take medicine and also reduces cholesterol and triglyceride levels and that subsequently prevents a bunch a pet owner from illnesses. Also dogs have been known to prevent skin conditions and allergies in children. Children who grow with dogs are less likely to have infections like eczema and also these children tend to have fewer pet allergies. Additionally, dog owners tend to recover from sicknesses than non-dog owners, these canines are amazing, aren't they?

When trained properly, dogs can serve as excellent service animals and can help people with disabilities tremendously. They can be taught to bring medication to their owners, they can detect when their owner is in discomfort and can even detect approaching epileptic seizures.

3 EMOTIONAL WELLBEING: THE PET SO-LUTION

A large part of this book will focus on the importance of dogs and other pets to the mental health of man. In this chapter, I will examine and highlight the things that happen when an individual is going to the negative sides of mental health (like trauma, depression and the likes).

For people going through depression for example, except the depression is very chronic, one can find gradual healing in pets. Wondering how this is possible? Let us look at a couple of ways that pets can take depression away because they tend to be able to effortlessly reduce tension around you and regularly improve your mood. Pets can be used to treat mild to moderate depression in the following medically proven ways. Firstly, pets can provide unconditional love to their owners and genuinely care for them especially for people with frayed relationships with friends and loved ones, when others fail then you can count on your dog to always be there for you and love you unconditionally. This assurance of unconditional love is key in the healing process for people going through depression. Secondly, most depressed people have the tendency to be covered up in bed or in their couches doing nothing and this might lead to worrying and other negative mental activities which might spell more harm for the victim of this mental downturn. Pets can help you out of this maze because owning one will definitely provide activity for you and you would always have something to do ranging from taking walks or tending to the dog or having a date at the vets or going to get food or clothing for the pet. All these activities will definitely widen your world view beyond the four walls of your home and keep you busy, these activities have been proven to improve physical and mental health in depressed people. Also, owning a pet will mean that you will create a routine because it is necessary to have one when you own a pet and when a routine is created for the dog, you also create one for yourself, this helps you look forward to every single day and gives you a very significant advantage in the fight against depression. Thirdly, one of the major effects of depression is isolation from the world around you and if this is done continually, over time it can lead to self-destruction. Owning a pet means that you are never alone and this companionship with the animal will make a positive difference. A fourth reason why it is important to own a pet in the battle against depression is that owning a pet has a special way of aiding social interaction. Pets can serve as natural icebreakers when it comes to interacting with others, you tend to meet people who think your pet is adorable or they have/had a very similar pet and so on. For depression patients, their social lives are nothing to write home about but statistics have proven beyond doubt that a pet can help you to connect more with others and create lasting relationships that are significant in the healing process for depression and other similar mental ailments. Also, most patients of depression really need to be reminded that they are capable, imoirtant and able to make positive and lasting effects on another being. Owning a pet is synonymous to being responsible for that pet and having a sense of responsibility will add a new focus to your life and increase your sense of value and importance. This new outlook has been described as very necessary by health professionals because it will help you in viewing yourself as very important and this will subsequently help you in the healing process. Although it might seem a little difficult or impossible at the beginning for folks that are depressed to take care of a pet but it is very significant and in fact it is a huge step in the right direction when that challenge is taken up and conquered. Another way to conquer depression by simply owning a pet is through the act of touching or being touched by the pet, it has been scientifically proven that physical contact is soothing and can help in numerous ways to overcome depression. There is a very soothing feeling that comes from petting you cat or having your dog sit on your lap, in fact it has been proven to reduce your heart rate. For people with some sort of severe sickness or infection like AIDS and so on, owning a pet can help you to deal with that reality better. It is normal for people in these kinds of situation to be prone to depression and stress but for pet owners it is not the case as pets will help you to take your mind off the disease.

The way stress works negatively in the human body can be likened to a state of disease as it is at this time that some harmful chemicals (like cortisol and norepinephrine) can negatively affect the immune system and make it vulnerable. Studies has successfully shown the strong link between the development of these chemicals and heart diseases. A way to tackle this problem is by producing chemicals like serotonin and dopamine which are proven to have effects of pleasure and calming the human mind. These chemicals can be gotten from consuming harmful drugs like cocaine and heroin which will in turn have negative effects on your health and on your finances. Similarly, these chemicals can be produced by simply playing with your pets, hugging someone you really love, watching the sunset with a loved one and so on. Pets are helpful beyond imagination when it comes to the mental health of humans. They can also help to distract us from the harsh realities that we might face and help us cope with and eventually overcome mental illnesses that prevent healthy lifestyles in humans.

Also, the difference between manageable and unmanageable anxiety in victims of mental disorders might simply exist in the fact that a person owns a pet, because pets have been proven to efficiently manage anxiety in victims, how? By just being there, quite amazing isn't it? But that is the magic that the presence of a pet can offer to victims that need support for emotional disorders such as anxiety, depression and the likes by being there for them when their owners become emotionally distressed. These pets have been known to help a lot of Americans that are going through these emotional rollercoasters and they are referred to as emotional support animals. An ESA (emotional support animal) does not require any training and can soothe the emotional upsets of his/her owner by being friends with the owner and helping them cope with their emotional issues. This ESA is different from a working service animal (as the latter is trained rigorously for the purpose of helping people with emotions). The difference is simply in the fat that the ESA is not trained and is a natural healer because by simply playing with or cuddling your pet, you will realize that animals have a great calming effect on people and they can help people dealing with the forms of anxiety, fear, depression and a handful of other negative mental emotions by helping to release our happy chemicals that help us battle emotions that negatively affect human mental health.

One major reason why people suffer these negative emotional downturns is because they do not live in the moment as they keep overthinking and causing more damage mentally as thinking often leads to ruminating over things that we probably would never get answers to. Often times we tend to set some unrealistic standards for ourselves and when we do not meet these standards we tend to become unhappy and hate ourselves because we feel that life is not the way it should be.

Dogs and other ESA pets can help to remain mindful and help us to focus on the present moment and subsequently make the best use of man's time, this will lead to a regular boost in such a person's mood and will subsequently result in the emotional stability of such a person. Mindfulness is a concept that as gained more prominence in recent discussions regarding man's mental health. By definition, mindfulness is the ability to live each moment as it unveils itself and to accept every moment without judgement. Being mindful has been proven to reduce stress in human and enhance man's health.

There are a lot of activities that enhances mindfulness and some of these include; yoga, massage, prayer, meditation and so on. One major activity that is highly underrated is the act of playing with/cuddling/touching your dog, cat or any other pet. There are certain mindfulness tips that can be learnt from a pet as pets do not care about plans that man as mapped out (that could at times make you feel like a zombie). Although it might seem like a disadvantage initially but looking at it closely, it has been known to help you to appreciate this factor and the reason is that it helps us to become unstuck from our mental shackles of how things should be and this helps us embrace distractions and embrace the fact that we are not in control of everything around us, understanding this will tremendously help in living a better life and letting go of preconceived ideas or thoughts on how we think things should be and makes us to see things as they really are thereby we get to accept the spontaneity of life.

Let us take a look at some ways through which pets can help us to remain mindful. Firstly, pets do not ruminate about the past and what could have happened or have sleepless nights because they worry about what the future holds (this leads to anxiety). Pets live in the moment and by living in the moment, you can overcome negative mental activities and stay focused on the present, believe me when I say that this has a lasting positive effect on your mental health. Another very important act of mindfulness that can be learnt from pets is the act of self-care, when we learn to take care of our physical and mental health, it puts us in the best position to fight anxiety and depression and helps us to stay happy. Do you ever notice how happy your dog gets when it is well rested or how cranky it gets when it doesn't get enough rest? It is the same thing for humans and if you do not take adequate and proper care of yourself, your mental wellbeing might be at risk. Another lesson that can be learnt from pets is that they can forgive easily. In forgiving people, you get to let go of feelings of anger and resentment which can have lasting negative effects on your mental health. Pets also teach us to make the most of every moment and by doing this we tend to bother about the most necessary things only. The most important lesson of all the lessons that can be learnt from pets regarding mindfulness is that pets teach us the act of self-acceptance which is key in the healing process or the total prevention of several mental ailments like depression, trauma and so on.

The negative effects of psychological disorders are nothing short of awful therefore, it is necessary to put in conscious efforts to prevent these ailments and a very easy way of doing this is by being a pet owner and you will enjoy the endless benefits of being around pets as these pets offer companionship, structure, affection and they teach us a lot of important life lessons. Therefore, if you feel like you cannot help yourself because you feel inadequate, you should consider adopting a pet because the advantages of owning one is higher in contrast to the cost of giving such a pet the good life that it deserves. Before we proceed, let us take out time in the next chapter to examine the relationship between man and animals and put it in a historical perspective to know where and how it all started.

4 ORIGINS OF THE HUMAN-ANIMAL RELATIONSHIP

It would be improper to say the least if I do not take a detailed look into the history of the man/animal relationship as I would look through the various stages- from prey/predator relationship to becoming an almost inseparable part of the lives of both the man and the animal. According to the theory of evolution, man is actually an animal that evolved through some stages over a couple of hundreds of thousands of years to finally arrive at what we are today (homo sapiens). Science holds this belief strongly and even believed that the current level of development that humans have attained once shared a common ancestor with what we call animals some million years ago. Scientists go further to say that man formed their own paths of evolution and based on fossils and skeletons found in some parts of the world, it as deduced that these skeletons showed both characteristics of humans and non-humans. In his evolu-

tion, man went from treetops to walking upright
and trying to make life easier for himself/herself
by using his/her hand to make tools and in the
production of things that keep humans alive. Then
came the stone age when humans used stone tools
and weapons. This tools allowed men to go
through the act of hunting.

At about 14,500BC there was a huge climate
change that made glaciers to cover most of the
land and this coupled with the fact that humans
were regularly hunting large animals led to the
shortage of food supplies for man and animals.
Large animals were driven to extinction at about
10000 BC and at this time, it is claimed that humans turned to hunting relatively smaller animals
and also man began cultivating plants. This major
shift had a very lasting effect on the human-animal relationship. Between the times of climate to
the extinction of larger game, man began to domesticate animals and set some animals apart
from wild ones. Man learnt 2 things during this
time;
- The taming of animals and
- The domesticating of animals
While taming simply involves rigorously training
a wild animal to behave calmly around humans
and subsequently do them no harm. Domestication on the other hand involves taming a while
species of animals over many generations so that
it becomes inherent for them to act calmly around

humans. Domestication is the reason for the proper coexistence of man and domesticated animals.

This difference between domesticated animals and their wild counterparts exists not just in the behavior but it also exists in the genetics of such animals (a factor/ quality such as size is a common denominator). This is probably what is responsible for the difference in the physical appearance in domestic and wild animals. The influence that pets exert on their owners is pretty amazing.

The history of the domestication of dogs as pets by humans can be traced as far back as 13,000 BC when humans started domesticating wolf-like species (canis lupus). Domesticated wolves helped man in hunting and shared the spoils, also they helped in man's security. Soon, man found dogs to be more hospitable and consequently domesticated dogs. In the case of the cat, scientists have found remains that are very similar to cat fossils. Although it is not a fact that these fossils belonged to domesticated or wild cats therefore it is safe to say that cats have been around humans since about 8,000BC. Most of the credit for the domestication of wildcats is given to the ancient Egyptian folks who have been domesticating wild cats since about 4,000 BC. It is very likely that they did that to secure their grains from rodents. This agricultural factor is believed to have highly influenced the popularity of domesticated cats at that period in time.

For livestock, it is believed that their domestication began between 9,000 and 5,000 BC, these dates were estimated based on evidence recovered from excavated archaeological sites.

Zooarchaeology or Archaezoology is the study of the history of the interactions between man and animals. Lot of clues have been recovered from the condition of animal remains found in and around human settlements.

For cows, pigs, goats and horses, their domestication came in particular order. First, the pigs were domesticated then cos and oxen then sheep and goats. History also has it that dogs assisted humans when it came to herding and controlling these livestock from the wilder animals. At about 6,000 BC, horses are thought to have been domesticated for their meat, skin and milk (as their milk was fermented into alcohol). From being used for their edible use, the relationship between man and horses got to the next level which as the level where horses were used for work- pulling carts, wagons and the likes-. Therefore, for the horse the advancement was from prey to working animals and then they were trained to transport things and in the act of warfare (because of their speed and stamina). The history of the domestication of the donkey can also be traced to the Egyptians at about 4,000 BC here they were thought to have been used as beasts of work to assist the oxen and subsequently, horses became riding animals and helped humans in the area of mobility and this helped immensely in trading between various societies and across various cultures.

The domestication of chickens can be traced to Asia at about 3,500 BC, they originated from the Asian jungle and they served as a means of getting meats and eggs for humans. Other domesticated animals and their estimated dates of domestication include camels who were domesticated around 2,500BC. Other domesticated animals include turkeys, ducks, guinea pigs and so on.

There were a lot of successful domestication tales of various animals by humans but a couple of them were not totally successful. A very significant examples from the group is the zebra. It was discovered that herdsmen from ancient times tried fruitlessly to domesticate zebras because of the multiple similarities that the striped mammal shares with the horse but in spite of these similarities with the horse, the zebra is genetically different from the horse (even though they can breed with horses). Zebras are known to be very ill-tempered when they are around humans and this as the main reason for the failure of man in trying to totally domesticate the mammal. Other animals that have never been domesticated include grizzly bears and buffalos. This is principally because of their lack of a proper social structure for domestication. Through history, the most suitable animals for domestication are those animals that naturally live in groups with a defined hierarchical social structure. In this hierarchy, man assumes the role of domination and to a very large extent he gets to control the behavior of the animal. This has become very evident in the evolving history of man/animal relationships.

It has been widely speculated that the coincidence between the rise of human civilization and the domestication of animals is because the animals served as a supplier of meat, milk and it helped man to give up his former nomadic lifestyle and helped him to fre his time to produce enough food for their consumption. This gave everyone free time to be productive and then humans started inventing, repairing and making great inventions.

As seen clearly in this chapter, the relationship between man and animals evolved from being just a means of feeding (sheep between 11,000 and 9,000BC and goats around 8,000BC) to becoming working animals (horses and donkeys between 6,000 and 4,000BC). This goes a long way in showing that man and animal have been in close contact with one another from time immemorial and both the man and his pets have mutual benefits that they enjoy and I would highlight these benefits subsequently in this book.

5 THE HUMAN-ANIMAL BOND AND OUR HEALTH

Through centuries, dogs have been said to be man's best friend (standing on all fours). Although more recently, more animals have been added to the almost unending list of man's favorite pets. As seen in the previous chapter, the relationship between man and pet blossomed over a long period in history and today it can be said that the relationship is at its most advanced level which is genuine friendship with mutual benefits. These pets provide humans with several emotional and physical benefits. The ability of pets (especially dogs) to form bonds with humans is nothing short of amazing. Pets can understand the mood of a person and subsequently decipher when something is wrong with that person and try (in their own peculiar ways) to make things right. Most pet owners can relate to a scenario when you arrive home to be greeted by the licking of your pet and you can sense the joy it has because

you are there. Most pets (especially dogs and cats) have been found to release the so called "cuddle chemical" (oxytocin) in both humans and pets. Briefly I ill deviate to have a critical evaluation of the functions of oxytocin in humans. Oxytocin is a hormone in the body that can do the following:
  - Facilitate the process of childbirth
  - Gives all round psychological stability
  - Increases trust and reducers fear.
Low levels of oxytocin on the other hand can lead to Autism.

The release of the chemical into both man and his pet is calming and it subsequently leads to having a stronger bond between them. The effects gotten from a dog's smiling face or from the entwining of your legs by your cat can help to lift your mood and get you relaxed after hours of work. Pets have not only proven to be very adorable but also very useful to humans psychologically, physically and socially. I will look at the benefits of pets on all aspects of man's life.

Pets have numerous benefits that they offer to humans. Firstly, they help in the reduction of blood pressure by helping your body to release a relaxation hormone and subsequently reduces the level of stress hormones. Also, pet owners are known to show improved success rates from heart surgery and are quicker in the process of recovery. Owning a pet also reduces cholesterol levels, triglyceride levels and so on. These terms might seem like medical jargons but to put it in simplest terms, pet owners are less likely to have heart disease mainly because pet owners enjoy physical activities with their pets. Also, those that own pets tend to be less likely to experience symptoms of depression because owning a pet contributes immensely to the improvement in the mental health and it also leads to a significant increase in the physical activities and social interactions of pet owners. Pets are known to reduce stress and loneliness thereby reducing the risk of experiencing depression or its symptoms.

For people who are feeling low, pets can serve as a source of inspiration or motivation to do things. Pets will help you to "draw" from your 'spring of strength' and get things done instead of just staying lazy. Pets (dogs especially) can serve as an incentive to go out and once this becomes a habit, it has a huge positive impact on your overall wellbeing. Also, pets can help you to stay calm when indoors with you (the company of another creature can help you to be calm).

When it comes to child development, pets can help in several ways to ensure the proper development and growth of children. Pets Can play a vital role in a child's social and emotional development by helping to improve self-esteem, autonomy and so on It has been proven that children who own pets have self-confidence, self enhancement, increased trust and so on.

Over time, it has been emphasized that man is a social animal that cannot exist without other people. Pets can serve as a social enabler for pet owners by ensuring that their owner is socially healthy, how? Firstly, animal clubs and societies that fight for the rights of animals brings about several opportunities for pet owners to meet and interact and share a wide range of ideas. Also, pets can help to improve the emotional bonding between members of a family. Pets are a magnificent catalyst when it comes to meeting people, networking and so on especially for people who live alone or those who have a difficulty in meeting other people.

Pets also have health advantages that are mot restricted to their owners alone. These ways of improving man's psychological health are more popular with dogs but can be done by some other pets also and it is referred to as Animal assisted therapy (AAT) in which people of all ages with disorders try to seek a return to normal mental health. Examples of these include increased eating habits, morale and overall health in Alzheimer patients. Also, having a dog (for instance) in waiting rooms has been proven to reduce annoyance and irritation between patients. Pets can successful serve as a form of distraction from the harsh reality of some patients and subsequently providing comfort and support for patients (examples include stressed out students, veterans and so on)

Some other benefits of pet ownership include fighting allergies. Research has proven that growing with pets gives strength to the immune system thereby helping that child to build immunity against bacteria. Another benefit that comes with being a pet owner is the improvement of one's emotional health. The most emotionally healthy people have attributes such as resiliency, confidence and the ability to develop healthy relationships and studies have shown that pet owners share these same attributes when compared to non-pet owners

As much as humans love to worry about the future or the past, pets help us to remember to live in the present because that is the only way they know how to live. Learning to do this keeps us in the present and helps us focus on making the best of every moment that presents itself. Also, pets Can help owners to create a sense of purpose. By creating a regular routine for various activities for your pet is very beneficial for the general well-being of such person because research has it that everyone needs something/someone to care for. Owning a pet, apart from its social advantages helps to reduce the frequency of of trips to the doctors (most times by just being the amazing beings that they are). Also, pets tend to be totally loyal to their owners and they love and care for them unconditionally and although they do not get to live as long as humans on the average, the death of a pet hurts badly and provokes and outpouring of grief (that is traditionally associated with the demise of a human being). This is one of the fe downsides of owning a pet and although it hurts to lose them subsequently, it is more important to enjoy their benefits while they live because pets are essential and their importance cannot be overemphasized.

There are numerous factors that should be considered when thinking of getting a new pet. I will end this chapter by stating some of these factors. They include;

- Level of commitment to taking proper care of the animal and perform essential tasks.
- When going for a pet it is essential to consider one's lifestyle and how it will affect your relationship with your pet. There are a wide range of options to choose from therefore it is necessary to choose the breed that fits into your way of life.
- Before adopting a pet, it is important to have a home that is pet friendly and get rid of hazardous objects that will hurt or wound your incoming pet(s).
- Always choose the best food that is appropriate for your pet's age and breed.
- It is also important to interview veterinary doctors before deciding on which pet/breed of pet to adopt.
- Adopting a pet is not enough, the pets needs thorough training to be able to adapt to the new environment

- Ensure that you select the appropriate toys
  for your pet (to prevent discomfort and in-
  juries to the pet
- Get your pet a proper identification to prevent it from going missing (and in cases
  where the pet is missing, the I.D helps to
  have your pet returned to you)
- Cost is probably one of the most important
  factors to consider before adopting a pet, to
  ensure the proper day-to-day healthy living
  of your pet

6 ANIMALS AS THERAPISTS

Through history, animals have been a significant part of human experience and existence and they have served various purposes through time. From the earliest times of being prey to becoming man's friend but most recently, animals (especially dogs) have been used for therapeutic purposes and although it was initially received poorly but subsequently, more healthcare practitioners have embraced animal assisted therapy (AAT) for patients.

By definition, animal assisted therapy also known as pet visitation therapy is a scheduled encounter with a qualified therapy team (an animal and its handler) for the purpose of helping patients to function maximally in their social, emotional and physical aspects. AAT can be done with domesticated pets (dogs, cats, guinea pigs and so on), farm animals (horses, pigs and so on) marine animals (dolphins). Dogs are the most commonly used pets when it comes to animal assisted therapy The whole essence of AAT is to provide an experience centered on the person (patient) that can increase health and wellbeing by lowering blood pressure, decreasing the level of anxiety, reducing loneliness and depression and improve the patient's mental outlook and the overall quality of life.

Animals who formerly shared traits with present day humans have been together for over 50,000 years and domestication occurred about 15,000 years ago. Pets that were domesticated served many purposes which included the roles of scavengers, objects of worship and food while some took up roles guards and soldiers. It was the late 1800s that a certain nurse discovered that small pets were very helpful in the reduction of anxiety in children and also adults who lived in psychiatric institutions this led her to conclude that being with small animals can help patients in the process of recovery. From here, AAT grew to become a more popular means of treating anxiety and furthermore as a way to relax. Animal-associated therapy is more than just petting animals. It goes way beyond that. AAT interactions are directed to meet a particular goal that is set for an individual. This process is directed by a human health professional and should be documented frequently to monitor progress in the patient. Health practitioners all around the world have described the results as excellent and have scored AAT very high. An example of an instant where

AAT can be used is when a child has gone through terrible events like the death of his parents or sexual abuse for instance. This child might be threatened by the appearance of the therapist but if a dog is brought into that scene, the child will probably loosen up and would mostly rather talk to the dog about his experiences (while the therapist listens). This is an example of a particular approach and there are more examples with other different methods and even though the methods might differ, the objective/ goal of AAT remains a constant. Dogs are the most common animals used in ani al assisted therapy. It is necessary to note that other animals can be also used (based on individual preferences). A therapy dog can be defined as a canine that is properly trained to show affection, love and comfort to people (for example people in retirement homes, hospitals and so on). Typically, these therapy dogs work side by side with their owners/ trainers who know them perfectly. There are various types of therapy dogs. The following shares some common examples.

Therapeutic visitation dogs which are household pets that are taken to places to act as a form of relief. They are taken to hospitals, adult homes and other places that has people in need of special psychological attention and are away from their homes for one reason or the other. These kinds of visit go a long way in helping an individual to erase stress and help them feel alive. With time, the visits become a part of the people so much so that they tend to look forward to it as it has positive effects on them. Closely related to therapeutic visitation dogs are disaster relief dogs and these dogs also bring comfort to people who have gone through some sort of psychological/ mental distress.

Facility therapy dogs are dogs that live and ork in nursing homes and are used in helping patients' recovery from mental and psychological ailments

Animal assisted therapy dogs are the ones that assist therapists in trying to ensure the total and prompt mental and physical recovery of patients. Most times, these dogs work in rehabilitation centers.

The last type I will be evaluating are the reading therapy dogs and they help children that have issues with reading in schools and libraries. Here the child is not bothered about his self-esteem as the dog creates an avenue to read and not be judged. Doing this ill subsequently make the child's reading skills to become better and also increase the child's confidence while ensuring that the child is excited about reading and would probably look forward to reading sessions with the pet.

The question might arise about the size of the dogs that will best suit the role of therapeutic dogs. Although it preferable to use smaller ones that are easily carried and held by patients las though they were little kids. Other factors asides size will include the canine's temperament. Some of the best breeds of dogs that can serve as therapy dogs include; Chihuahua, corgi, French bulldog, beagle, greyhound, poodle, mastiff, pug, dachshund, and so on. As long as a dog can pass the necessary tests then it can act as a therapeutic dog.

Therapy dogs should be well socialized, they must be well-tempered and they must love to make other people happy.

7 THE UNIQUE BOND BETWEEN PEOPLE AND DOGS

There seems to be a natural tendency for humans and pets to form a relationship with one another, even if the animal is not that individual's companionate animal, or "pet". This natural tendency may be what fosters such genuine friendship or companionship between man and his best friend on four feet- the dog. Dogs have been said to possibly be the best pets when it comes to therapeutic uses by humans not only because of their intelligence and compassion but because they have been known from tie immemorial as man's best friend.

More recently, dogs have been used for more than just companionship as the have been seen as a solution to some mental and physical problems and this has in more ways than one helped to further tighten the bond between man and dogs as it evolved from just a physical relationship to becoming more emotional in nature.

This evolvement happened through years of co-operative cooperation and mutual benefiting which involved an increase in trust and affection between both beings that has made the animal-dog bond to become deepest between man and any of the other lower animals. This bond was further fueled by certain human characteristics like the need to nurture, this need is very intense so much that it could lead to health deficiencies in humans if the need is not properly met. Apart from this, dogs have always helped the better man's ability to express love and affection and this has been proven to improve mental health and they are a great social and physical motivation, dogs have increased the quality of life by significantly reducing depression and loneliness which is the root cause of most mental ailments in humans.

This bond doesn't just provide joy and happiness, it also provides a range of several other health benefits for not only the man but the man and his canine companion. From mere petting your dog, you can significantly reduce blood pressure and heart rates in both the man and the canine. All neurochemical and positive hormones are positively affected as a result of this amazing bond. Stress reduction is another amazing outcome of this very mutually benefitting bond. It also brings feelings of comfort to humans as it has been proven that humans can function better in the presence of their dogs. There are other benefits from this bond which include increase in plasma concentration of beta-endorphin and dopamine and a real reduction in stress levels and a change to certain physical features that have been associated with relaxation.

The amazing benefits of the emotional and physical bond between man and dogs also include certain therapeutic uses which entails providing emotional support, friendship and psychological healing for folks that need it, other chapters of this book have captured this therapeutic relationship between man and dogs (other pets are also included sometimes)

The unconditional love that dogs have towards us helps to further facilitate this bond as time goes by and these canines have continually shown that they are beneficial to our health by reducing blood pressure and heart rates and helping us to live better lives. These canines have really impacted our lives in very positive ways through this bond and we happily look forward to more amazing years, decades, centuries and millennium of sharing in this amazing bond!

8 ANIMALS AND TRAUMA RECOVERY

All through this book, I have shown the importance of pets in several areas of man's mental health and the usefulness of pets cannot be over emphasized, in this chapter, I will take a detailed look into the importance of animals in trauma recovery while looking at some real life examples, but before that I will like to briefly explain what PTSD is.

PTSD is an acronym for Post-traumatic stress disorder, for people who have experienced some sort of life threatening ordeal (an accident, assault, abuse, war and so on.) it is common to experience trauma and other mental health deficiencies which can be handled by professionals but often times it happens that these signs and symptoms linger for months after the treatment of the trauma. For cases like this, it is necessary to seek medical help again as that is the beginning to PTSD and although it cannot be totally cured, it can be contained and the patient will get to live a

very normal life afterwards. For better understanding, I will use a certain illustration of a sol-
dier who just returned from war and after some-
time trying to resettle with the normal lifestyle,
he still has difficulties in aligning to the normal
way of life. For this person (let us call him Paul),
being in a crowded place will make him uncom-
fortable as he will be too self-conscious and
would not feel safe seeing so many people around
him. Also, Paul can hardly sleep and when he
manages to, he is restless and cannot enjoy his
sleep. For Paul, he keeps having flashbacks of
the terrible things he has seen especially when he
sees something that reminds him of the traumatic
event. Paul will of try to avoid situations that he
thinks will cause him to remember stuff therefore
he withdraws from the world and enjoy solitude
and might result to alcohol or drug abuse. Also, as
a result of the things Paul might have seen in the
times of war, he might feel worse about himself
and the world at large and he would have trust issues and he might find it hard to be happy. Also,
it will lead to Paul being easily irritable he would
get angry over little things, he would always be
on the lookout and he might experience shock due
to loud noises, sudden movements and so on. The
above illustration is a typical situation with
someone suffering from PTSD.

Over the last several decades, a number of
reviews regarding the state of research in the animal-assisted intervention (in the treatment of

PTSD and other traumatic ailments) have been conducted. For example, in 1984 reviewed claims of therapeutic benefits of pets in addition to the earlier research approaches testing hypotheses that were presented. Their findings noted the primary use of descriptive methods of research in earlier research that not only lacked real evidence of a successful running of such approaches with real examples. In the year 2008, 129 studies were reviewed that examined the effects of both pet ownership and animal-assisted activities/animal-assisted therapies conducted since 1980 to determine whether any changes were in place. Since that 1984 review, they found that while most research continued to be descriptive, a greater number of experimental studies had been conducted. Their conclusory findings stated that a few pockets of evidence do exist and appear to be growing, Pets appear to reduce the impact of stress on patients as I would look at some practical examples later on in this chapter.

Further compounding the lack of significant empirical support for the benefit of animal-assistance in psychologically therapeutic contexts is the lack of consistent findings among the existing research that may already bring with it limitations and flaws, based upon its less empirically robust nature. For example, in 1975 it was found that having companionate birds increased social interactions among the elderly. Similarly, decreased levels of depression and anxiety was found among individuals living in an institution or singly who had contact with a therapy dog or companionate animal, yet their data were derived from self-reports, which is not a 100% acceptable source and might offer threats to validity as well. However, some other researchers found no differences in perceived happiness, psychological well- being, or loneliness amongst study participants with companion animals and those without, but the researchers relied upon limited empirical approaches. Despite the limited empirical support, the benefits of including canines in treatment continues to be very promising as more practical situations have been used to show such benefits.

It is important to set a variety of treatment goals in therapeutic work involving animal practitioners. These goals span across things such as improving social skills, enhancing affect and mood, the provision of pleasure and affection, potentially improving memory and recall, and coping more effectively with grief and loss, enhancing self-esteem and self-worth, improving motivation for cooperative interactions with others, improving concentration and attention, decreasing manipulative behaviors, and improving ability to express feelings, reduction in general anxiety and hyper-arousal, opportunities to engage in appropriate physical contact, and working toward a reduction in abusive behavior are likely to benefit from canine co-therapists. Likewise, improving ability to trust and improving problem-solving ability may be facilitated by the use of pets especially dogs in psychotherapy. Many of these potential goals correspond directly with the therapeutic needs of individuals engaged in psychotherapy for the relief of traumatic symptoms that often bedevil them. As a result, the contributions of therapy dogs in psychotherapy for trauma recovery might provide potentially advantageous clinical gains. However, the ability of the affected individual to obtain each of these worthy goals awaits empirical confirmation.

A number of techniques have been outlined that might be facilitative in contributing to these types of possible treatment outcomes. Such techniques may suggest that the therapy animal providing clinical services along with the clinician might engage the clients in an appropriate manner to do two things, firstly, to explore clinically significant issues and to address them. It is possible that with a variety of intervention options, clinicians could use clinical judgment to select and tailor strategies for helping patients make strides towards trauma recovery based treatment goals. Examples of techniques include the following with clinical illustrations to follows:

- Giving and receiving affection with an animal through petting or holding the animal
- Learning gentle ways to handle an animal; learning to communicate effectively with an animal

- Better understanding about how animals learn things using various techniques
- Observing and discussing animals' response to human behavior via examining immediate consequences
- Generalizing animal behavior to human circumstances
- Learning about proper care, feeding, and grooming of an animal
- Engaging in appropriate play with the animal
- Talking to the animal or discussing the animal
- Learning and repeating information about the therapy animal as well as other animals
- Requesting the animal to do tricks or commands it has learned
- Teaching the animal a new trick or command
- Following a sequence of instructions with an animal
- Taking the animal for a supervised walk
- Introducing the animal to others
- Discussing how an animal might feel in certain situations
- Learning about and discussing or contemplating animal behavior
- Developing a cooperative plan to accomplish something with the animal

Each of these activities within the framework of therapeutic work targeted toward clinical gains may facilitate a greater connectedness of a trauma patient to his lost selfhood. This may be done either through corrective use of an animal as a self-object, the regaining of a sense of empowerment or connectedness with another, or through increased self/other awareness with the animal therapist acting as mediator.

In addition to these therapeutic interventions, it was further espoused that a number of more projective animal-assisted tasks and interventions might be employed. These techniques may involve distancing negative experiences from traumatized clients so as to perhaps remove threatening or overwhelming internal experiences with the use of therapy animals as possible self-objects, whereupon such experiences may be projected in a safe manner. For instance, storytelling with the animals experiencing similar events, cognitions, or emotions might facilitate clinical work. Similarly, use of illustrations and coloring based on animals may provide clinically significant projective information that might then be used in conjunction with verbal therapeutic interventions. Such strategies might be particularly beneficial in working with traumatized clients who may have difficulties tolerating the accessing and engagement of negative and distressing internal states, such as anxiety, often accompanying trauma recovery. Furthermore, such activities facilitate rapport building between therapists and clients as therapists may convey regard for clients as well as animals, or the particular therapy animal, while conveying a nonjudgmental stance.

The negative effects of PTSD have been stated earlier in this chapter and to help veterans who are going through mental downturns, The United States Military and Veterans Affairs have also recognized the unique role of dogs within the lives of traumatized individuals in the process of total recovery. Various Organizations have been created to help soldiers who might be suffering from various degrees of trauma and these organizations provide selection and training of service dogs for veterans dealing with combat-related Post Traumatic Stress Disorder. In fact, Paws for Purple Heart, an example of organization created to help military men has partnered with Palo Alto/ Menlo Park VA Medical Center, Walter Reed National Military Medical Center (Bethesda, Maryland), the National Intrepid Center of Excellence, and Fort Belvoir for operation of its intensive service dog training centers. The organization notes that these service dogs have a very huge chance to contribute to decreased trauma symptomatology among veterans with service dogs. Although the role of a service dog is more integrated within the life of a handler than that of a therapy dog, the benefits of a service dog within the management of trauma-based symptomatology may be paralleled within the therapeutic relationship through clinical interventions and practices

Some real life examples include:

A former captain in the U.S. Army, recounts his experiences recovering from the debilitating effects of his own complex-PTSD symptomatology with the help of a well-trained and provided service dog called Tuesday. These service dogs are trained individually to potentially target the specific symptoms each veteran presents. In the case of this captain, he grappled with symptoms brought on by his recurrent exposure to combat trauma. He described the relationship with Tuesday as possibly instrumental in facilitating his re-engagement in life activities during a time when he did not trust human beings. Gradually, as the veteran's relationship with Tuesday developed, the Captain describes what has been referred to in the literature as emotionally corrective experience, and he began rebuilding his life. The captained mentioned that the dog changed the quality of his life, it reminded him to cake medications, helped him tackle social agoraphobia (the fear of the onset of a panic attack and appearing distraught in public), hyper-vigilance and flashbacks. He said the dog made him became the happy, loving and adventurous person that he used to be.

In a similar manner, military serviceman David Sharpe shares his story of recovery from debilitating combat trauma-based symptoms and the significant role his dog, Cheyenne, played in his recovery. The veteran's trauma-related emotional downturn led to outbursts of anger, alienating others from his life, until he noted the perceived impact of his fits of violence on Cheyenne while she was in the periphery. Sharpe recounts that Cheyenne appeared to respond in a manner that demonstrated "knowing something was wrong with him" because pets have feelings too and most of them understand us perfectly. Compelling the veteran to seek comfort from her. He described an experience of positive emotional relief and significant changes following his experiences with Cheyenne. It appears that the affiliative bond between the two may have contributed to his sense of relief as well. Based on his experiences, the veteran founded Pet2Vet, a non-profit organization that provides other military servicemen with companionate animals. Pet2Vet has provided companion animals to hundreds of veterans with compassion for the animals in mind as well by ensuring that the pets provided are rescued or from shelters. In fact, it is not just to the advantage of humans but selection in this manner contributes to animal welfare.

From victims of sexual abuse to the ones that were neglected in childhood to the veteran that lost his sense of connection to selfhood and so on. The journey is indeed a very rough one as it is not an easy feat to climb from the shackles of trauma into leading a normal life but the integration of pets (especially dogs) is helping people to recover from these mental health downturns. Real life examples have proven beyond any form of doubt, the efficiency of animal assisted treatment for trauma and it these pets have not only saved lives but also helped people to get back on track and reconnect with the the world around them

The possible integration of animals in the psychotherapy of trauma recovery will require not only clinical skills but also animal-handling skills. Thus, it is essential that, with such extensive preparation and training involved, therapeutic techniques involving the use of therapy animals be adequately efficacious as well as effective. For this reason, it is recommended that a set of guidelines for treatment with this special population be devised by a competent and credentialed mental health professional uniquely tailored to each case.

9 CONCLUDING THOUGHTS

All through this book we have taken a critical look at the importance of creative, adorable, intelligent and very loving creatures that we take as pets and we have seen numerous ways that these pets have helped the human race. Pets serve as an intrinsic part of our lives and basically the affect every part of our lives from the moments when we crawl up until we grow old enough to die.

Animals love us unconditionally and they are loyal to a fault when the need arises. These lovelies can help reduce pressure in us and keep us calm, safe and socially involved with other people. Asides these regular uses (which prevent the 'special cases' from occurring), these pets can be used in the process of recovery from certain mental ailments like Trauma, depression, loneliness and so on. The idea is not to replace human relations with animal relation but to ensure that the animal aids and improves relation with other humans and help to change your view of the world totally. There have been several cases where pets have saved lives and helped people speed up down the path of recovery from mental ailments to the path of recovery. These pets (companion pets) have a way of making you to become positive and very social. They will motivate you to go on about with youthful activities. The joy on the faces of your pet is immeasurable when you walk past your door, these pets genuinely love you!

Do you know that your pet can also help your marriages? Research has it that newly married couples with pets feel more satisfied with their unions, especially if they both love pets. These animal will serve as a means of connecting for the couple before they begin to have kids, by both caring for their furry 'children'. These animals reduce stress levels between partners in a marriage and help form strong social relationships with others. Generally, these pets just make us happier not forgetting their usefulness when it comes to recovery from ailments too.

The importance of pets can never be overemphasized and I think everyone or at least every family should have one of them because pets can almost do no wrong.

ABOUT THE AUTHOR

Dr. Sally Nazari is a licensed psychologist practicing in the Hudson Valley of New York City and Boston metro area. Following her practice as a master's level social worker, she went on to attain master's and doctoral degrees in clinical psychology with distinction as well as advanced certifications in Cognitive Processing Therapy (CPT) for PTSD as well as in Dialectical Behavioral Therapy (DBT). Dr. Nazari first explored animal connections as a young child with the local strays and exotic animals in cartoons. Eventually, her interest in psychological and holistic approaches of the human-animal bond grew into research along with a number of mainstream and scholarly publications. She has also been invited to author multiple publications in Tier 1 peer-reviewed journals, 17 internationally recognized professional presentations, and hold leadership positions within professional organizations. Dr. Nazari has also been a sought out featured speaker and trainer in such facilities as the New York Presbyterian Hospital, Helen Hayes Hospital, Good Samaritan Hospital, law enforcement communities across three states, and school districts on a variety of topics. Additionally, she is a topic expert within the Good Therapy community and has been interviewed in multiple international print, digital, and on-screen media outlets. She also contributes regularly to two regional publications and is currently broadcasting the *Beyond the Couch* podcast. Dr. Nazari emphasizes holistic approaches in enhancing the wellbeing of those she works with in addition to the animals in their lives by offering a range of integrative and holistic healing modalities in her psychotherapy practices. In addition, Dr. Nazari works as a psychology associate professor to educate undergraduate and graduate students in counseling and psychology. Her life is enriched by the love and joy from her beautiful animals as well as the ones she serves on a daily basis.